Reckless Abandon:
A Study in Surrendering It All to God and Resting in His Peace

Alyssa J Howard

ISBN-10: 1981898395
ISBN-13: 978-1981898398

CONTENTS

Introduction

LIVING A LIFE OF RECKLESS ABANDON

Do you trust God? I mean REALLY trust Him? Do you serve Him with reckless abandon?

What if He asked you to do something that seemed utterly crazy to the people around you? What if following His lead meant taking a risk? How would you feel if trusting Him in an area of your life meant turning your world upside down? The Bible is full of stories of men and women of God who did just that. Noah, Abraham, Esther, Ruth, Mary and Joseph... They all took great risks for God and threw worldly caution to the wind. I think of Gideon who told a majority of his army to go home when he was about to face one of the greatest armies in the world at that time. Everyone must have deemed him a fool. *But he trusted God and was given a mighty victory.*

When someone lives a life of reckless abandon, one of two things is happening. Either they are foolish and prone to making bad decisions that have dire consequences. Or they know something that the people around them don't know. In this case, what seems like a reckless decision is actually a wise one.

As Christians, we are children of God. We have been given God's peace beyond understanding as well as His promise to work all things together for our good. *In other words, we have something that the world doesn't have...*

"I have one desire now - to live a life of reckless abandon for the Lord, putting all my energy and strength into it." - Elisabeth Elliot

- **Throw worldly caution to the wind...**

We use the phrase "reckless abandon" to describe a life or a decision where someone abandons all common sense. It may seem reckless and possibly even dangerous. We make decisions that in the end, could be harmful to us in some way. *But the truth is that when God is involved, no decision is reckless. When we are following God's lead, nothing is a risk.* The world may look on and call you foolish, but you know in your heart that you are living in God's peace and wisdom. He will never lead you astray.

- **Leave your worries behind.**

Jesus commanded us not to worry about anything. God is a good Father who takes care of His children. So when it comes to your finances, He's got it covered. When it comes to your family, He's got it covered. And when it comes to your day-to-day life and concerns, He's got all of that covered too.

It's time to recklessly abandon our worries once and for all and trust God fully to do all He has promised in our lives.

Do not be anxious about anything, but in everything by prayer and supplication with thanksgiving let your requests be made known to God. And the peace of God, which surpasses all understanding, will guard your hearts and your minds in Christ Jesus. - Philippians 4:6-7

- **Abide in God's peace beyond understanding.**

This truly is the number one key to living a life of reckless abandon for God. *You cannot abandon your earthly worries unless you replace them with the peace of God.* Again, the world may call you crazy for being at peace in the midst of a trying circumstance, but God's peace transcends all worldly understanding.

You keep him in perfect peace whose mind is stayed on you, because he trusts in you. - Isaiah 26:3

Serving God with reckless abandon is only possible when we are willing to abandon our worldly concerns and replace them with His peace beyond all understanding.

Unit 1: Defining God's Unconditional Peace

DO YOU DESIRE TO HAVE PEACE BEYOND UNDERSTANDING?

Do you long to experience God's peace? I think it's safe to say that we all desire peace in our lives… but peace beyond understanding is something entirely different. *God's peace is beyond understanding because the world can't understand how we can be at peace in the middle of a storm.* And let's face it. Storms happen. There's no such thing as a life without hardships and struggles. So when God promises us peace in the midst of these trials, it's a promise that seems almost too good to be true.

In this way, His peace is unconditional. It is not dependent upon the condition of our lives at the moment, but rather it is dependent upon the fact that we are abiding in Him.

If you truly desire to have peace beyond understanding, there are three biblical truths you must realize…

- **True peace comes from God alone.** Apart from Christ, we can experience *moments* of peace. After all, no one lives in a constant state of emotional and physical storms. There are moments in life when all is going well and things are working out as planned. *And then it happens… the storm comes.* For most, finding peace when things are going well is easy. But the storm makes it hard… nearly impossible in fact. How do you experience peace in chaos? You simply can't apart from Christ.

- **Peace has nothing to do with calmness, rather it's your state of mind in the midst of a storm.** When the disciples found themselves in the middle of a storm on a boat with Jesus, they were anything but peaceful. In fact, they were panicking for their lives. Jesus, on the other hand, was asleep. (Now that's peace beyond understanding!) When the disciples woke Jesus up, His response was somewhat surprising. He actually rebuked them for being frightened! In all honesty, there was no reason for them to be afraid. Jesus was with them in that storm, so there was no justifiable reason to be scared. How often do we find ourselves fearful or worried in the midst of a "storm." Jesus is with us too. In fact, our hope in Him is described as an anchor for our soul (Hebrews 6:19).

- **When we abide in the peace of Christ, we demonstrate to the world what life is like as a child of God.** Peace is a fruit of the Spirit. In other words, when we are allowing the Holy Spirit to work in our lives, peace is naturally produced. What does it say about our faith when we live a life of worry? We tell others they can trust God and experience His peace, but then we vent our fears to our friends as if we have no hope. *In this scenario, our words and our actions don't align.* While it's okay to confide in a trusted friend for encouragement and prayer, it's not okay to spread hopelessness and fear.

God doesn't simply want us to experience His peace beyond understanding, He desires for us to live in it.

True peace beyond understanding has nothing to do with what's going on around you... so if you find you're only at peace when things are going well, you aren't experiencing God's true peace.

Now may the Lord of peace himself give you peace at all times in every way. The Lord be with you all. - 2 Thessalonians 3:16

WHY YOU NEED GOD'S PEACE TO ACCOMPLISH YOUR DESTINY

If I were to ask you what it takes to accomplish your destiny, what would you say? What first comes to mind? Hard work. Dedication. A plan of action. What about peace? Does peace even come to mind? Probably not. But the truth is that God's peace is an essential part of walking in our God-given identities. And if you're not walking in your true identity, accomplishing much for the Kingdom will be extremely difficult... if not impossible.

- **We never accomplish much in the midst of chaos.** I see this in my own life in a very physical way. When my house is in disarray, I struggle tremendously with my to-do list. I don't even know where to begin! But when I work in a clean and organized environment, something just clicks. I can think more clearly and accomplish so much more in the process. Now, I can't promise you there won't be chaos in your life. Sometimes our struggles feel like a tornado of debris swirling around us. But that's the beauty of God's peace. It surpasses all understanding and allows us to think clearly... even in the storms of life.

- **When we abide in God's peace, we are able to focus on what really matters.** A while back, my hometown experienced a severe wind storm. The power outages alone were astounding. (Ours was out for five days... many endured longer.) I remember looking outside at the massive pine trees near our home. I was so worried they would come down, as many of the trees in our neighborhood had. Meanwhile, my family was inside the house trying to find light, heat, and food. What was truly important in that situation was for me to be a mother to my children - to calm their fears and to feed them. But instead, I stared at those trees in worry. More often than not, we do this in our own lives. We allow our fears to distract us from what we should be doing.

If you want to accomplish your destiny (and I assume you do), you need to be able to focus on the things that matter most. Storms have a way of stealing our attention. Don't let them.

- **When we choose peace, we are choosing to rely on His strength and provision rather than our own.** The Bible teaches us that God's peace is freely given to all who become children of God. It is a naturally produced fruit of the Holy Spirit in our lives. So for the Believer... peace is a choice. We can choose to abide in the peace God has given us, or we can live in a place of worry and fear. I don't know about you, but choosing peace is something I have to do throughout my day. But I am finding that the more I choose to abide in His peace, the easier it becomes to live in it.

Tackling your work is so much easier when you're well rested. We accomplish so much more! And not only do we accomplish more, we tend to do so with joy in our hearts... we actually enjoy our work when we are working from a place of rest. (Some would argue that working from a place of rest isn't really work at all!)

This is one of the reasons why God's peace is so important. He longs for you to work while abiding in His peace so that you can accomplish your destiny in Him.

When we are resting in God's peace, we are able to accomplish even more for His glory.

THREE REASONS WHY PEACE AND JOY GO HAND-IN-HAND

One thing we all have in common as human beings is our desire for happiness. Sure, we may go about it differently. Some of us try to find it in relationships, while others look to a career or financial security to provide happiness. Either way, we all want to be happy. But did you know that peace and joy go hand-in-hand? Think about it this way. *If you are uneasy or stressed it is much harder to be truly happy.* More often than not, joy and contentment work together in our lives.

So why bring up joy in the middle of a study based on peace? The truth is that many of us search for happiness, but what we don't often realize is that peace is a major part of that puzzle. Stress, worry, and anxiety all have a way of trying to rob us of our joy. But when we choose peace... we can expect joy as well.

May the God of hope fill you with all joy and peace in believing, so that by the power of the Holy Spirit you may abound in hope. - Romans 15:13

- **Peace and joy come from the same source.** The Bible tells us that both joy and peace (along with many other blessings) come from the Holy Spirit. When we are abiding in Him and allowing Him to work in our lives, we can EXPECT fruit. *They are naturally produced in our lives.* That being said, I'm not sure we can experience true peace or joy separate from one another. After all, they are BOTH the result of abiding in Christ. We may experience moments of "peace" or "happiness" apart from the Holy Spirit. But in Him, we can expect to live in TRUE peace and joy... the kind that isn't based on circumstances.

- **When we live in God's peace we experience His joy.** This is something I've been personally working on in my own life. In my quest to find happiness, I often forget that abiding in God's peace and rest is essential. Can you imagine no longer feeling worried or stressed? How much joy are we missing out on when we choose to focus on our circumstances rather than surrendering them to God?

- **Faith and trust** *produce* **peace and happiness.** We already know that abiding in Christ produces peace and joy in our lives. But what does that look like in practice? *We choose to abide every time we make the conscious choice to trust God with our lives.* When we are experiencing financial difficulty, we choose to trust that God will meet all of our needs. When we are suffering from a painful loss, we surrender our pain to our heavenly Father. And when we are worried about everyday circumstances or safety, we know that God is watching over us in every way.

When we choose to place our trust in our heavenly Father, we can expect to experience His indescribable peace and joy.

Unit 1 Study Guide:

1. Read Mark 4:35-41. What do you notice about the fear of the disciples in this passage? What do you notice about the peace of Jesus?

2. Based on the events found in Mark 4:35-41, what connection do you see between faith and fear?

3. List some ways that unrest (or a lack of peace) keeps us from our calling in Christ.

4. According to Philippians 4:6 and Isaiah 26:3, what are some practical ways to handle unrest in our lives?

5. Based on John 15:4-5, what is the key to producing fruit in our lives?

6. Read John 14:27. List some key differences between the peace this world offers and the peace only Jesus can provide.

7. Personal Reflection: What do you personally hope to gain from this study on God's peace?

8. Prayer: Ask God to show you the areas of your life that desperately need His peace. Spend time thanking Him for His amazing gifts.

Unit 2: Discovering Peace in Your Day-to-Day Life

PEACE IN YOUR MARRIAGE

Marriage is bound to have moments of unrest. It doesn't take long after the wedding day to figure out that marriage can have its share of difficulties. It's inevitable for every couple to disagree or argue. But what if I told you that peace was indeed possible in your marriage?

Now, I can't promise you a marriage without fighting. Every marriage, even the best ones, will deal with complications and disagreements. But living in unity and peace have nothing to do with fighting or not fighting. *It's how we deal with these disagreements that make or break the peace in your marriage.*

I could give you some practical marriage advice for when both parties are in agreement. For example, any married couple who has been happily married a decade or more will tell you that forgiveness is essential. Also, praying together and openly communicating are crucial parts of any godly marriage. But what do you do when your spouse isn't in the "communicating" mood? How do you find peace in your marriage when it feels like it all depends on you?

- **Entrust your entire marriage to God.** This feels like such a basic principle, yet it can be difficult at times to put into practice. In good times and in bad, God longs for you to have an amazing marriage. How do I know this? Well, the Bible tells us that marriage was designed to be a reflection of our relationship with Christ. *We are His bride.*

- **Walk in peace in your *own* heart and life.** If you truly want to find peace in your marriage, you have to put forth the effort to abide in God's peace in your own personal life. Let me put it this way. When I'm struggling with worry and fear, I tend to take it out on my husband. I'm not *trying* to do this... it just happens naturally. But if I surrender my personal worries to God, I have a better chance of keeping peace in my marriage.

- **Do *everything possible* on your end to live in peace.** The Bible tells us to live in harmony with everyone... to do everything within our power to keep peace in our relationships. Obviously, there are times when we've done all we can and the other party refuses to do their part. But it is our responsibility to do everything on our end. So often, we think to ourselves, "I'll put forth effort when they start putting forth some effort" or "If only they would try harder, I would try harder." *But if both spouses are thinking this way, how will peace ever be achieved?*

- **Rest in God's peace even if your marriage is in a state of unrest.** The best part about the peace of God is that it transcends all understanding. In other words, God's peace trumps our circumstances. We can experience the peace of God even when things are less than ideal. So when your marriage is in a place of unrest, you can find rest in your Savior's arms.

When abiding in God's rest, peace in your marriage is indeed possible.

FINDING PEACE WHEN YOU'RE RAISING LITTLE ONES

My life before children was rather quiet. *Calm. Peaceful.* Sure, at the time I would have said that I was busy and things were chaotic. But I had NO CLUE what I was in for when I had two little girls 19 months apart. My life was suddenly much different. One baby was easy compared to two... I loved these little human beings more than anything. *But how was I going to survive raising little ones?!*

I have many mommy friends. And honestly, I don't know how some of them do it. I see their pictures plastered on social media... all happiness and giggles. Everyone looks so calm and put together. I mean, how on earth do these moms do it? Four little ones at the fair?? I could barely get my two to church on time!

Now, perhaps you don't currently have little ones in your home. But many of us do have young children in our lives in one way or another. Grandparents, single parents, honorary aunts and uncles… kids are simply a part of everyday life. My girls are older now (six and four at the time this is being written). And even though things can still get crazy, I've learned a lot.

- **Have a plan.** When you "wing it" each day, it's easy for the chaos to become too much to handle. When my girls were really little, this definitely looked more like a schedule than a routine. I needed some structure to keep my sanity! But now we have found a rhythm. I'm no longer looking at the clock, but we definitely have a sense of routine to our day. I also try to plan activities and fun to make each day special.

- **Activities, activities, activities.** When my girls were really little, I found myself trying to *survive* the day... so much so that I wasn't enjoying them the way I wanted to be. So we started doing more and more activities. Instead of sitting in front of a television screen, we are playing with play-doh, coloring, crafting, practicing our "letters," etc. And when all else fails (and when the weather cooperates), we have a picnic outside!

- **Take time to focus on them and get to know them personally.** Before I was a mom, I taught dance at a local studio. I loved working with the little ones especially. (Three and four year-old-girls have the funniest personalities!) But when I had my own children and life was crazy at home, it was easy to become so preoccupied with dishes and laundry, that I didn't take the time to get to know my own girls and all of their funny quirks. I knew I needed to make a change, and I am so glad I did! I'm still their mom, but I'm also their friend. We talk about life, which is a habit I want to continue as they get older.

- **Surrender the chaos to God.** When all else fails, take the chaos to your Father. He knows you and your children better than anyone else. He knows exactly what everyone needs in the most chaotic of moments. Let Him fill your heart with peace, inspire you to be creative, and strengthen you to maintain your patience in every circumstance.

God promises to be our peace... even when raising little ones who are less than peaceful!

TRANSFORM YOUR HOME INTO A PLACE OF PEACE

Do you ever feel like your days are non-stop go, go, go until bed time? Oh my goodness! How I feel this way on most days! We have our to-do lists that are a mile long. House cleaning, cooking, homeschooling, kids' activities, family time... we all have our "stuff" that keeps us busy. *But is this the way God intended for us to live our lives?*

I know I try to fit too much into my schedule. It doesn't take a rocket scientist to figure out that I have more on my daily to-do list than I have time for; but even then, I feel like I'm non-stop going even on the days I don't have too much to do. Perhaps it's our culture... always on the go... always moving forward at a crazy pace. God promises us peace in our lives, and I honestly believe that extends into our home life. *He longs for our families and our homes to experience His peace, which is one of the reasons He tells us to seek and pursue it. (1 Peter 3:11)*

- **Simplify your life.** When it comes to our culture, we are far from simple. We have a billion and one ways to connect and interact with each other. We are all trying to keep up with each other when it comes to the latest trends. And don't even get me started on Pinterest... as a mom, I love getting ideas, but sometimes I feel like I can't keep up with the new standards of mommy-hood. A birthday party is no longer as simple as balloons and a cake. I have to have a theme and elaborate decorations!

When I say it's time to simplify, I mean it's time to not only simplify our homes but also our schedules and our expectations. I don't have to keep up with every other mom (who is probably running herself ragged anyway). I don't have to have the cleanest house of all my friends. And I certainly don't need to fill my day with activities for the sake of activities. I, for one, long to return to the days of simple.

- **Have a routine but know when to be flexible.** I LOVE having a routine to my day. This became especially true when I first had my girls. But often I let my need to have a schedule take precedence over everything else. *I become a slave to my routine... so much so that I struggle with stress when I stray from it.*

- **Make home a cozy place.** My daughters love to be "cozy," and they love to come home after a long busy day. Our homes should feel like a safe place. It's where we can put our feet up and truly be ourselves. Of course, this will look different for everyone. Perhaps you make your home cozy by making sure it's organized and de-cluttered. Maybe you enjoy having music playing or having a scented candle lit. I have found that keeping the television off makes a huge difference. Too much background noise definitely makes things seem more chaotic! In the end, it's about enjoying all of the "cozy" things that God has blessed us with.

- **Make memories every. single. day.** It's so easy to let a day go by and consider it to be just another "normal" day. But the truth is that there is no such thing as a "normal" day. Each day is a gift from God. We can choose to make memories and take advantage of each moment or we can speed through our day... the choice is ours to make.

God calls us to walk in peace in every aspect of our lives, including our homes. After all, He is our refuge and our safe haven.

HOW TO KEEP PEACE WHEN IT COMES TO YOUR FAMILY

You don't get to choose your family. I can clearly see this truth in my daughters. When my youngest daughter was born, she was born into an already established family with a built-in big sister who didn't like her much at first! Now, they love each other. They fight like sisters naturally do, yes. But they miss each other desperately when they're apart.

As we grow older, our families become more complicated. We gain more and more extended family members, and people go through "phases" of life that can sometimes be not so pleasant to witness or endure. Unfortunately, tragedy can strike, bad decisions are occasionally made, and feelings are sometimes hurt. So what then? How do we handle these things as a family? *How do we keep peace as Christians?*

- **Walk in love and compassion... always.** The love that Jesus talked about and lived out was radical, to say the least. He dined with sinners... Now, this may not seem like a big deal today, but in their first-century culture, it was a VERY big deal. No religious leader would have been caught eating at the same dinner table as a known criminal or sinner. It was a social no-no.

Jesus' mission was His first priority. Above all else, He loved people regardless of their past or present. He longed to give them a future in Him, and the only way that would be possible is if they knew His love.

As children of God, we have experienced His love for ourselves. But the Bible is clear that we are now called to share that love with those around us. And this mission should be our first priority... especially when it comes to our family members.

- **Turn the other cheek.** I will admit... this one is incredibly hard. Even under Old Testament Mosaic Law, they weren't required to forgive in this manner. But Jesus changed the game...

"You have heard that it was said, 'An eye for an eye and a tooth for a tooth.' But I say to you, Do not resist the one who is evil. But if anyone slaps you on the right cheek, turn to him the other also. And if anyone would sue you and take your tunic, let him have your cloak as well. And if anyone forces you to go one mile, go with him two miles. Give to the one who begs from you, and do not refuse the one who would borrow from you." - Matthew 5:38-42

Think about this one for a minute... Jesus is saying something quite radical in this passage. I'll be honest, no one wants to be a doormat. *Even Christians should have limits... right?*

We need to remember one important thing. **We, as believers, have the power of the Holy Spirit in our lives.** Our flesh will always crave an "eye for an eye." Living a life that turns the other cheek requires us to rely on the Holy Spirit in a supernatural way. We need God's perfect love to flow through us. Our imperfect, human love isn't enough to live the way Jesus outlines in this passage.

Let me challenge you with this: What if every single believer lived their lives this way? What if we truly loved in this manner? What kind of impact would that have on the world? On our families?

- **Pray for them.** It's easy to love those who love us. It's harder to love those who hate us or have wronged us in some way. Anyone can love someone who is nice to them. But only someone with the love of God inside of them can truly love someone who hates them. The key to loving those the world would deem "unlovable" is prayer. When we pray for someone, our hearts change. We begin to see them through the eyes of God. *And in His eyes, no one is unlovable.*

Remember... Every single member of your family is loved by God.

I truly believe that God puts people in our lives for a purpose. We are called to influence and love, and this begins at home. We are all at different points in our journey. Your family members may be hurting or going through difficult circumstances. They may be mean or lash out. And sometimes... they are just difficult to be around. But God's love carries us through. It transcends all things and has the ability to heal in ways that nothing else can.

Unit 2 Study Guide:

1. According to Romans 12:18, how are we called to live our lives when it comes to earthly relationships?

2. You may or may not currently have little ones at home. If not, can you think of any practical advice you could share with a young mother in your life? If you do have young ones, what are some real-world ways you can create peace at home for yourself as well as for them?

3. Read Proverbs 1:7 and 24:3-4. What do these passages teach regarding our homes and how they ought to be built?

4. List some practical ways you can simplify your home and create peace.

5. Read Luke 5:30-31. What was the mission of Christ and how should this affect our attitudes towards difficult family members?

6. According to Matthew 5:9, 43-46, how does Jesus describe the "sons of God"?

7. Personal Reflection: What area in your day-to-day life needs God's peace the most? Identify some practical ways you can work towards peace in that area.

8. Prayer: Ask God to show you someone in your life that desperately needs God's peace. Spend some time in prayer asking Him to show you how you can be a peacemaker in that person's life.

Unit 3: Is Financial Peace Possible? And If So... How?

THREE REASONS WHY TRUST IS THE KEY TO PEACE IN YOUR FINANCES

How much time do you spend worrying about money? If we're being honest with ourselves, we probably worry about it more than we realize. Every time a bill is due or something needs to be repaired, we worry. We stress. Even when things are going well financially, there's always something that comes up. Or maybe you spend your days worrying about savings and retirement. Truth be told, money is a universal issue. Every person on the planet will have to come to terms with it at some point. Perhaps the real issue here though has nothing to do with money at all. More money doesn't equal more peace. *But what if I told you that peace in your finances was possible?*

- **God promised to meet all of our needs.** The Bible is FILLED with promises concerning God as our provider. He takes care of His children and meets their needs both physically and spiritually. And not only do we have promises, but we have examples. God provided manna for the Israelites in the wilderness. He sent ravens to Elijah each morning and evening with bread and meat to eat. And when the crowds were hungry, Jesus miraculously provided food for thousands. *All of this proves that God cares deeply about our physical needs.*

For some reason, it's a lot easier to trust God in spiritual matters than physical. I can trust Him for peace and guidance, but I have a much harder time when I need to trust Him with my grocery budget. But Jesus was pretty clear in His teachings, however, that it is the Father's heart to take care of His children's needs.

Look at the birds of the air: they neither sow nor reap nor gather into barns, and yet your heavenly Father feeds them. Are you not of more value than they? - Matthew 6:26

- **Jesus commanded us not to worry.** If this isn't a reason not to worry, I don't know what is! Worry is actually a sin. When I first realized this truth in my own life, I was immediately convicted. Think about it this way... worry is simply a lack of faith that God is who He says He is and that He will provide for us the way He promises in His Word. *It's doubting the very character of God.*

- **Worry doesn't improve anything... and that includes your finances.** Has worry ever achieved anything for you in your life? Does worrying about your life, your health, your kids, or your career amount to anything? Why do we think that worrying will help things? It won't. Jesus said so.

And which of you by being anxious can add a single hour to his span of life? - Matthew 6:27

If you keep telling yourself that you'll be at peace when your finances are secure... you will never be truly at peace. Because even the wealthiest of men could have it all taken away in an instant.

In the end, financial security doesn't exist, but financial peace is possible when we place our trust in a God who provides for His children.

THREE WAYS THAT GIVING WILL INCREASE YOUR FINANCIAL PEACE

Would you consider yourself to be a giving person? I'm not talking about making charitable donations or giving to your church, but rather the overall picture. Many will give to things they believe in or give in their abundance. But "givers" are a different breed. They naturally give of themselves in every circumstance. Givers have no problem surrendering their time, their skills, and their resources to meet a need in someone else's life. And while many of us have no problem giving in our abundance, givers make sacrifices. They give even when it's hard. Some would say it's not financially smart to sacrificially give, but what if I told you that being a giver would *increase* your financial peace?

- **Giving helps us to recognize what is truly important in life.** Stuff isn't important. People are. When we become givers, this truth becomes even more apparent in our lives. *Our finances become less important, while the Kingdom becomes our focus.*

- **When we give, we begin to see the world the way God does.** Throughout His ministry, Jesus saw needs and met them. He couldn't help Himself. He saw people with compassion, longed to meet them where they were at, and desired to meet their needs in a supernatural way.

- **Giving demonstrates the heart of God to others.** Our Father is a Giver. He provides, heals, and restores... and He gave His only Son to give us the right to become His children. When we give to others, we are demonstrating what true love looks like in action.

Believers are called to give for many reasons. It helps us, helps others, produces growth, demonstrates love, meets needs, etc. In the end, however, we are called to give because God first gave for us. *For God so loved the world that He gave...* He didn't reluctantly give, rather He gave with love in His heart.

So how does all of this help you increase your financial peace? It comes back to the source of your giving. *Are you giving with God's love in your heart? Do you rely on the power of the Holy Spirit to guide you in your giving?* **And most importantly, does giving come naturally or do you find it to be difficult?**

That last question is a hard one. Most of us aren't naturally inclined to sacrificially give of our selves... and I'm not just talking about finances. Our time and our resources are often hard to give away. It becomes even more difficult when we feel taken advantage of... no one wants to feel like people are using them.

Let me ask you a question... do you think every person who came to Jesus did so with the right motives? Do you think people ever took advantage of His heart and ability to perform miracles? The Bible tells us that Jesus even felt compassion for those who rejected Him... even those who plotted to kill Him. But for Him, giving wasn't work; rather it naturally flowed from His heart towards the people He loved.

Are you a giver or a taker? Takers rarely experience financial peace and security... they are always trying to get ahead and hoard what they have. They feel entitled and see the world in terms of what they can get out of it. Cheerful givers, however, do experience financial peace because they realize that everything they have belongs not to them, but to God. They allow the peace of God to rule in their hearts rather than worldly possessions.

But here's the secret to becoming a giver: Don't try harder to give more. Instead, allow the Holy Spirit to work in your heart to transform you into a person who naturally gives.

And above all these put on love, which binds everything together in perfect harmony. And let the peace of Christ rule in your hearts, to which indeed you were called in one body. And be thankful.
- Colossians 3:14-15

If you long to increase your financial peace, allow the Holy Spirit to transform you into a cheerful giver.

WHY STEWARDSHIP PLAYS A SIGNIFICANT ROLE IN FINANCIAL PEACE

Money is one of the most difficult topics to discuss in the church. *Why is that?* After all, money is universal to everyone. Seriously... everyone on the planet uses some form of exchange system to buy and sell. Yet for some reason, we get really uncomfortable. Perhaps it has to do with ownership. We all feel inclined to believe that our money belongs to us alone. We get to decide what to do with it. And to some extent, that is true. God cares deeply about ownership. In fact, many of the laws He gave Israel in the Old Testament placed an emphasis on rightful ownership. But in other ways, we need to remember where our true treasure lies. The things of this world are just things, and in the end, it all belongs to the Creator. *As Christians, we are called to stewardship rather than ownership.*

The earth is the Lord's and the fullness thereof, the world and those who dwell therein. - Psalm 24:1

- **Who is the owner of all things?** I think we all know the answer to this one. God created the whole world and everything in it. It all belongs to Him. The Bible calls us "stewards." Interestingly enough, our stewardship is rarely mentioned in terms of money; but rather we are stewards of all that God has given us... including the earth. Think of it this way. Adam and Eve were placed in the Garden of Eden, and they were put in charge. It was Adam who named every animal on earth. Fast forward to the New Testament when Jesus gave us the parable of the talents. Each person was given talents (money) to manage while the owner was away. And they were held responsible for what they did with those talents. Our families, our homes, our gifts and abilities, *and our finances...* they all belong to God and we are called to manage them wisely.

- **What is our role as Christians?** Stewardship is a high calling. In essence, God created the world and made us its managers. That's a big job title! Jesus also put us in charge of His Kingdom. We are called to spread the Gospel and expand the Kingdom far and wide! When it comes to stewardship in our finances, we often struggle with the idea that we don't "own" what we have rightfully earned. But as we can clearly see in every other aspect of stewardship, it's a high calling that shouldn't be taken lightly. We are entrusted with all that God has given us.

- **How should this affect our spending habits? Our giving?** If someone asked you to take over their finances for a month, how would you view that money? If it were me, I'm fairly certain I would put a significant amount of thought into how their money was being spent. I would be smarter and wiser because I was being trusted to do well. I would also have no trouble doing what was best with those finances, even if it was hard. Why? Because it's not my money. If the person who trusted me with it asked me to give some of it away, I would do so with no hesitation because the money truly belonged to them. *That's how it is with our finances... Our finances belong to God.*

When we remember that we are stewards first, it takes the pressure off of us. I can trust that the Owner of my finances knows what's best. (And He does because He knows all things - right?) Stewardship also requires us to work smarter and harder. We aren't frivolous with something that doesn't belong to us in the first place. We budget, and we plan for the future.

Stewardship brings financial peace because it takes the responsibility off of us and gives it to the true Owner of all things.

FOUR TRUTHS THAT WILL TRANSFORM YOUR BUDGET
(AND PROVIDE PEACE OF MIND)

Before my husband and I were married, we took a well-known course concerning our finances. We learned all of the best ways to plan a budget and save for retirement. And while all of it was wonderful and practical, I couldn't help but wonder if, in all our financial planning, we'd forgotten how much the Bible has to say about the matter. Nothing this course taught was unbiblical. In fact, the teacher himself was a Christian. But the truth is that no financial planner or well-executed budget can prepare us for every life event. We plan and prepare, but no amount of planning will give us true peace when it comes to our money.

- **What does the Bible say about wealth?**

This is undoubtedly one of the most controversial topics in the church today. While some pastors teach that God longs for us to be prosperous and wealthy and that He wants to bless us financially "beyond our wildest dreams," others teach that a Christian's life is marked by poverty and surrendering everything to God. *But what does the Bible teach?*

There are many stories throughout the Old and New Testaments of righteous men and women God blessed financially. Abraham and Job were both prosperous when it came to finances, and it's clear that God blessed them *because of their favor and righteousness in Him*. But then there are stories of those who suffered. Many of the earliest believers shared their belongings with one another and gave well beyond their means on numerous occasions.

One thing the Bible makes clear is that it is not a sin to be wealthy. And it is also not a sign that you lack God's favor or adequate faith if you're in a season of financial need. As Christians, we are called to be content and to find our strength in Christ who meets all of our needs. Paul said it best when he claimed that in any circumstance, wealth or poverty, he was content. In every season of life, he knew that it was God who gave him strength.

- **What does the Bible say about giving?**

Giving is another topic of controversy in the church. Unfortunately, many preachers have distorted biblical truth in order to gain for themselves. This was even prevalent in the days of Paul and the New Testament. (2 Peter 2:1-3)

Here are three truths about giving we learn in the New Testament:

1) We are called to give cheerfully and not reluctantly. (2 Corinthians 9:7)

2) It is our responsibility as Christians to take care of those in full-time ministry. (On a side-note, Paul gave up his "right" to make a living as a minister of the Gospel. This doesn't mean we shouldn't pay our pastors. But it does demonstrate the heart of a true minister. His heart was first and foremost to share the Gospel, even if it meant sharing it for free.) (1 Corinthians 9:3-18)

3) We are called to follow the Holy Spirit's lead when it comes to giving and to give according to what we have. This truth somewhat contradicts some of the teachings I've personally heard about giving in your poverty. Unfortunately, I've heard many teach that we can "give" our way out of debt. Yes, there were times in the Bible when people gave beyond their means and God blessed them because of their obedient and willing hearts. (And I firmly believe that God honors ANY heart that longs to please Him in their giving.) But these examples were the exception, not the rule.

There may be times when the Holy Spirit asks you to give sacrificially and trust God to provide. But this is not the standard of giving Christians are called to live by all the time and in every circumstance. Paul made this clear in his second letter to the Corinthians when he told them to give cheerfully according to their means.

- **What does the Bible say about planning for the future?**

There are numerous passages in the book of Proverbs that discuss financial planning. It is wise to work hard and make a living. But there definitely needs to be a balance. Work hard, yes, and enjoy the fruits of your labor, but not to the point where it becomes your everything. Treasure in heaven is far more valuable than wealth on earth.

Do not toil to acquire wealth; be discerning enough to desist. - Proverbs 23:4

- **What does the Bible say about financial security?**

The New Testament makes one thing abundantly clear: *true security comes from Christ alone.* Having peace in your finances is only possible when we stop worrying about money and instead trust God to provide. We work hard, give to those in need, and trust Him with the rest.

We learn to be content in every season of life, and in this way we rest in His peace.

When it comes to financial planning and creating a budget, it's crucial to keep these biblical truths in mind. The goal of any budget should be to honor God first and foremost. Be wise. Listen to counsel. Plan for your future. But don't allow money to rule your life. As Jesus said, we can only serve one master.

Making the choice to honor God with your finances will transform your budget in a way you never dreamed possible.

Unit 3 Study Guide:

1. What does Matthew 6:30-32 teach us about trusting God with our basic needs?

2. Read Proverbs 19:17, Luke 6:38, and 2 Corinthians 9:6. What basic principle about giving do we see throughout the Bible?

3. According to 1 Timothy 6:17-19, how should we handle our earthly wealth? What is the true definition of financial security based on this passage?

4. Read Matthew 25:14-30. What do you learn from this parable about our role stewardship role on this earth?

5. What does 1 Timothy 6:6-8 teach us about contentment and wealth?

6. According to 2 Corinthians 8:7-15, what should giving look like in the church today?

7. Personal Reflection: Take some time to reflect on you relationship with money. Is it where you find your peace and security?

8. Prayer: When Jesus said that you cannot serve two masters, He was referring to trying to serve God and money at the same time. Spend some time in prayer asking God to help you rely on Him fully for your peace and financial security.

Unit 4: Finding Peace in Our Relationships

PEACE WHEN IT COMES TO YOUR FRIENDSHIPS

From an early age, we all seem to have a desire to make friends. Even my young daughters crave relationships in their lives outside of their immediate family. As we grow older, however, we learn that friendships can be both rewarding and painful. Experiencing peace when it comes to your friendships is sometimes easier said than done.

- **Remember the purpose of friendship.**

1) Companionship/Love - We were created as relational beings. Even in the Garden of Eden, God said that it wasn't good for man to be alone. As relational beings, we all desire to love and to be loved. It's a built-in need that friendships meet in our lives.

2) Encouragement/Strength - As we go through life, we will experience hardships and trials. But friendships give us the strength to endure. We can lean on each other as we go through difficult times, and we can be each other's strength when we feel we can't go on. We also support one another as we help our friends who are going through things we ourselves have already gone through.

3) Accountability/Growth - The Bible tells us that as iron sharpens iron, we sharpen one another. (Proverbs 27:17) Perhaps this is the part of friendship we struggle with the most. *Growth is essential, but it can also hurt.* Iron sharpens iron through friction. It's necessary, but the process isn't always fun. We are called to keep each other accountable as we serve Christ, and challenge one another to grow... even when it's hard to hear.

Recalling the true purpose of friendship helps us keep things in perspective. We not only remember what it means to BE a friend, but we remember that friendships take effort. Experiencing peace when it comes to your friendships requires you to be selfless in your thinking. You give instead of taking, and you forgive instead of becoming bitter.

- **Do EVERYTHING you can to keep peace.**

If possible, so far as it depends on you, live peaceably with all. - Romans 12:18

1) Seek forgiveness when necessary. - It's hard to admit when we're wrong. Humility is definitely hard when we have to face the consequences of our actions. But nothing destroys friendships faster than pride.

2) Turn the other cheek. - When someone hurts us, it isn't generally our instinct to put ourselves in a position to be hurt again. But this is exactly what "turning the other cheek" looks like. Now, Jesus wasn't saying that we should set ourselves up for a beating, but we are called to forgive unconditionally the way we have been forgiven by God... and that requires vulnerability. Our sin hurts God, it actually grieves the Holy Spirit. Yet when we come to Him for forgiveness, He doesn't put up a defensive wall just in case we decide to hurt Him again in our sin. *He welcomes us with arms open wide.*

3) Make every effort to restore relationships. We have all been hurt by people we love because the truth is that people are imperfect and will fail us. At the same time, however, we must remember that we are imperfect too. We fail the people around us all the time. With all of this "failing" going on, it's easy to see why some people give up on friendships altogether. *But this is not how Jesus called us to live. The world will know we are His followers by our love for one another.*

Now, there are a few exceptions to consider... God never intended for us to be the victim of abuse. It's simply not His character. Sometimes, it is best to distance yourself from an abusive situation. *But we are not off the hook when it comes to unconditional forgiveness.* Another exception is the friend who refuses to make peace, even when you are making an effort. We can't control the actions of others, only our own. This is why Paul said "If possible..." when speaking of peace in our relationships. We are simply called to do all we can on our end.

- **Surrender broken friendships to God.**

There will be times when we do all we can, and restoration is simply not possible. But that doesn't mean we can't have peace. True peace comes when we surrender our hurts and frustrations to God. Our friendships are no exception.

The world knows that we belong to Jesus by our love for one another. That is why it is so important for you to have peace when it comes to your friendships.

HOW TO HAVE PEACE WHEN A LOVED ONE DOESN'T KNOW JESUS

One look at the title of this section and you're probably thinking to yourself, "No way. Not possible." Is it really possible to have peace when a loved one doesn't know Jesus? *Well, it may depend on your definition of peace...* For the Believer, following Christ is a matter of life or death. Knowing that a loved one has rejected Jesus is not only difficult emotionally, but it can also cause strain on your relationship with that person. You so desperately want them to know God's love the way you do, but they want nothing to do with it. Trust me when I say that I understand... *it's hard.*

- **Know that it isn't up to you.** I think we often put undue pressure on ourselves when it comes to reaching the lost for Jesus. Yes, we are His hands and feet, but I think Paul said it best in his letter to the Corinthians:

I planted, Apollos watered, but God gave the growth. So neither he who plants nor he who waters is anything, but only God who gives the growth. He who plants and he who waters are one, and each will receive his wages according to his labor. For we are God's fellow workers. You are God's field, God's building. - 1 Corinthians 3:6-9

So while we are all God's workers called to spread His Good News, it is the Holy Spirit that miraculously transforms lives causes growth. Think of it this way... when you plant a seed in the ground, you are the one doing the planting. *But then you have to walk away.* You have no role whatsoever in causing that seed to sprout and grow into a plant. In the same way, we are called to spiritually plant seeds and water, but God does the rest. So don't be discouraged if you don't see growth yet. *Seeds sprout underground long before you see the results above ground.*

- **Surrender your loved ones to Jesus.** What do you do when you have done all you can to reach the people you love, yet they refuse Jesus over and over again? There's not much you can do on the surface. Pushing too hard never works, and it will strain your relationship. The only thing left to do in this situation is to surrender them to Jesus.

We do this in two ways...

First of all, pray for their eyes to be opened to the truth. In other words, pray that God will reveal Himself to them. Truth be told, He knows much better than you do about reaching them the way they need to be reached. He knows their hearts, so He knows what they need to see and hear.

Secondly, surrender your worry to God. I, for one, know what it means to worry about my loved ones. I want what's best for them, and I wholeheartedly hate watching them suffer without Him. But all of this worry isn't good. In fact, God commands us NOT to worry about anything... and that includes the salvation of family members and friends. Surrender them to God, and allow His peace to move in your life.

- **Trust God and His Word.**

The Lord is not slow to fulfill his promise as some count slowness, but is patient toward you, not wishing that any should perish, but that all should reach repentance. - 2 Peter 3:9

God's heart is for all to know Him... He longs to adopt every single man, woman, and child as His own. *Rest in this truth. Jesus died for the sins of the entire world so that all would have access to His saving grace. He longs to see them come to Him even more than you do.*

When a loved one doesn't know Jesus, we can have peace in knowing that God's heart is to see all come to Him.

NO LONGER UNITED: HOW TO HAVE PEACE IN THE BODY OF CHRIST

Scrolling through my online newsfeed, it's pretty clear that we are far from united. And I'm not just talking about our country... I'm speaking of the church. This division isn't new. Our church has always faced divisiveness; so much so that Jesus prayed for our unity shortly before His death and resurrection. *He KNEW that we would struggle to be united.* The good news is that peace in the body of Christ is possible through the Holy Spirit. We need to be united in Him. But how do we do that when we all have our varying theologies and ideals? How on earth are we supposed to get along?

We are the Body of Christ, and the Bible is very clear that we are all talented and gifted. God has called each of us to a unique purpose in Him and has equipped us to carry out that call. *But in the end, we are all different.* **Different isn't bad. Different is good.** In fact, it's how God designed us to function as a whole. A body cannot function with one body part. It needs many to complete even the most mundane of tasks. *Yet for some reason, we often try to function this way as the Body of Christ.*

Churches are everywhere. In my hometown, we actually have an intersection with three separate and very large churches on each corner. Do these churches ever co-mingle? Unfortunately... probably not. They are three separate denominations that generally don't get along. *This is such a shame...* They worship the same God, bow their knees to the same Jesus, yet they have allowed differing denominational viewpoints to keep them apart.

In fact, today's culture has taken denominational differences a step further. We now charge anyone with differing beliefs as a false teacher. Now again, I'm not talking about salvation issues here. Paul defined what it means to be a Christian in Romans 10:9-10.

Because, if you confess with your mouth that Jesus is Lord and believe in your heart that God raised him from the dead, you will be saved. For with the heart one believes and is justified, and with the mouth one confesses and is saved. - Romans 10:9-10

It's rather simple, don't you think? You don't have to be raised in a certain denomination, sing the right songs on Sunday mornings, or even dress a specific way when you gather together with other believers. A false teacher teaches a different Jesus, a different gospel, and generally does so for personal gain. (In fact, nearly every mention of false teachers in the New Testament refers to the teacher's heart and their motives rather than simply their bad teaching.) *To label everyone as a false teacher who teaches a theological view you disagree with only hurts the Body of Christ as well as our ministry to the world.*

Please hear me out on this one... theology is ever changing. Studying church history and what has been taught for the past 2000 years has opened my eyes to what it means to be a Christian as well as a theologian. You study. You debate. *And you respect differing viewpoints.* Why? Because I can assure you that no two theologians will ever agree on every aspect of Christianity. In fact, there were many church fathers who changed their viewpoints throughout their ministries!

If I were to tell you every single thing Martin Luther, John Calvin, Dwight L. Moody, George Whitefield, John Wesley, etc. taught in their lifetimes, I can guarantee you wouldn't agree with every single theological point. And I can say with certainty that they didn't (and wouldn't) all agree with each other. **Yet these men of God did tremendous things in the Body of Christ to further spread the Gospel and bring about revivals.**

Until Jesus returns, our theology will have its flaws... and until then, we cling to the simple Gospel truth and stop arguing over the little things.

So we come back to one specific question: how do we have peace in the Body of Christ?

- **We focus more on where we agree rather than where we disagree.** As Christians, we all have the same Holy Spirit living within us, bow our knees to the same Savior, and are children of the same Father. If we can find a way to be united in these truths, we will be unstoppable at sharing God's love with the world.

- **We stop slandering those within the Body of Christ who hold different viewpoints.** This one is incredibly hard for some... especially now that we have social media and can share our opinions anonymously. But how many battles are fought within the church over non-fundamental theological issues? Does your salvation really depend upon your view of how worship should be conducted? Or does it depend on your viewpoint of women in ministry? It's okay to know where you stand on an issue, but it's not okay to put others down who don't agree with you.

There is one body and one Spirit—just as you were called to the one hope that belongs to your call— one Lord, one faith, one baptism, one God and Father of all, who is over all and through all and in all. - Ephesians 4:4-6

It is only possible to have peace in the Body of Christ if we all choose to recognize that we are united in one faith, one Spirit, and one Savior.

FOUR WAYS TO EXPERIENCE PEACE IN THE WORKPLACE

Jobs come and go. If we're lucky, we will end up in a career we love. For the rest of us, our jobs simply provide a source of income. Wherever you fall on that spectrum, our jobs matter. We give a huge portion of our time to them. Even if we hate our jobs, they still matter. Why? Because our jobs do far more than put food on the table. We build careers, learn new skills, and form relationships. *And truth be told, peace in the workplace is essential because our jobs are such a huge part of our lives and our personal ministries.*

- **Know who you're REALLY working for...**

Whatever you do, work heartily, as for the Lord and not for men, knowing that from the Lord you will receive the inheritance as your reward. You are serving the Lord Christ. For the wrongdoer will be paid back for the wrong he has done, and there is no partiality. - Colossians 3:23-25

Now the above passage is directly speaking to slaves, not employees, but the principle remains the same. (*Note: Paul is not endorsing slavery here. He is speaking to the cultural fact of his day that many new Christian converts were slaves and had no idea how to behave towards their masters... especially masters who were cruel or unfair.*) This passage is clear: we work for God, not man. I also find it interesting that Paul addressed mistreatment in verse 25. We are STILL called to lovingly serve, even when being unfairly treated. Now that doesn't mean we have to stay at that job. Unlike the slaves Paul was speaking to, we have a choice to work elsewhere. But while we are employed, we must do all we can to represent Christ.

- **Understand the role your career has in your ministry...**

Many view their careers as just that... a career. But God is not in the business of wasting 40+ hours of your week! Your job is so much more than a job! It's the place God has called you to minister. Think about how many people you come into contact with each and every day. Now, this doesn't mean you have to witness everywhere you go. (You would potentially be fired for doing so!) But it does mean that you get to share God's love with everyone around you. You can LIVE out loud even when you can't SPEAK out loud.

- **Love EVERYONE you meet unconditionally as Jesus would love them...**

I can't tell you how many times I've heard people say that they hated their boss or a co-worker. It's almost a cultural thing... no one actually LIKES their boss, do they? The truth is that when they are not working with you at your job, your boss and your co-workers are everyday people. They go home to their families, deal with their share of struggles, and need the love of Jesus just as much as anyone.

- **Trust God with the rest...**

When your job is less than ideal... when your boss is on your case... when you're overwhelmed by your workload... when you're struggling to establish your career the way you want it... take it all to God. *Let Him handle the stuff you have no control over.*

The most important step to having peace in your workplace is to entrust every single aspect of your job and your career to God.

Unit 4 Study Guide:

1. According to Ecclesiastes 4:9-12, how valuable are our friendships?

2. What is God's role in bringing someone to Him? What is ours? (see 1 Corinthians 3:6-9 and John 6:44) How does this truth give you peace?

3. According to 1 Corinthians 12:12-27, how are we united as believers? How should we respond and interact with differing members within the body of Christ?

4. What are some practical steps we can take to be peacemakers in the Body of Christ? (see 2 Timothy 2:23-25 and Proverbs 15:1)

5. Read 2 Peter 2:1-3, 1 Timothy 6:3-10, and Ephesians 4:11-16. What do we learn about false teachers and their motivations? What motivates a godly teacher? How do we identify false teachers in the church today, and how should we respond as we strive for peace and unity?

6. Why do you suppose Peter encouraged his readers to honor those in leadership even when they were being cruel and unjust? (see 1 Peter 2:13-19) In what ways does this biblical principle still apply to us today?

7. Personal Reflection: Is there currently a relationship in your life that lacks peace? What are some practical steps you can take to restore peace in that relationship.

8. Prayer: Spend some time in prayer for a loved one who desperately needs Jesus. Ask God to help you with your role in bringing them to Him.

Unit 5: Resting in God's Peace When Your World is Less Than Peaceful

FINDING PEACE IN THE CHAOS (WHEN LIFE IS CRAZY BUSY)

When your life is crazy busy, how do you cope? How do you survive? No really. I want to know. Chaotic lives seem to be the norm these days. We are a culture on the go. Everything needs to be handed to us in less than five minutes. Why? Because time is valuable. And none of us seem to have enough of it.

When did it get this bad? Take moms for example. We are no longer allowed to simply be good and caring moms who love and raise our children well. We have to excel at planning activities, packing extravagant school lunches, coordinating after-school schedules, cooking like a gourmet chef, and planning themed birthday parties that are over the top and ultra-creative. *How do we find time to be moms (or even decent wives) in the midst of all this coordinating and planning?*

I firmly believe that busyness was never God's plan for us. This is clear throughout His Word. He so desperately wanted to spare us from a crazy busy life that He established an entire day of rest at the beginning of creation! When was the last time you ACTUALLY took an ENTIRE day off from any and all work?! Most of us can't even fathom it. Even when I'm spending a "family" day at home, my day is spent cooking, cleaning, and prepping for the work week.

So how do we cope when life is crazy busy?

- **Learn to say 'no.'** This step is so practical and so simple, yet many of us don't put it to use. Perhaps you need to say 'no' to that additional activity for your children. Or maybe you need to step back from a commitment that is consuming your time and leading to unrest in your life. *If you're anything like me, learning to say 'no' means learning to be content when I can't get everything done on my to-do list.*

- **Find your strength in God.** Sometimes we can't say 'no.' Sometimes we are faced with a crazy time in our lives that is beyond our control. When my second daughter was born, I was faced with such a time. To say my life was crazy busy would be a serious understatement. I had an 18-month old daughter and a fussy newborn to take care of... I was exhausted. It was in these moments that God taught me to find my rest and strength in Him.

- **Lean on loved ones for support.** We are called to be united and to encourage one another towards growth in Christ. And through it all, we are also called to be present in each other's lives. God gave us each other to rely on in difficult circumstances. He never intended for us to go through life on our own.

When life is crazy busy, we need to take it to God.

Because in the end, it is His strength and His wisdom that we can rely on to bring about peace in our lives.

HOW TO KEEP PEACE ON SOCIAL MEDIA (AND WHY IT'S ESSENTIAL TO YOUR FAITH)

Since I began studying God's peace beyond understanding, I have both anticipated and dreaded this particular topic. If I'm being honest, it was social media that first inspired this study. Our culture is most certainly at war... one that is readily seen online. We fight battles each and every day from the comfort of our own homes and often anonymously. *Is it even possible to keep peace on social media?*

I wish I could say that I only saw this sort of thing from those who don't claim Christianity. But unfortunately, I can't. In fact, some of the cruelest things I see online come from those who subscribe to a faith that is supposed to be based on God's love... a faith that should be known for its morals and integrity.

Social media is a wonderful tool. We can communicate in a way we never dreamed possible. I can keep in touch with those who are far away, see pictures and videos of my nieces and nephew, and keep up on the latest news and trends. But social media has a built-in flaw... anyone can post nearly anything at any time... often with little to no consequences. We can be mean, slander those who disagree with our viewpoints, post our opinions on every major and minor topic, and spread news stories that offer very little in the way of credibility.

This has caused many to question the use of social media altogether.

I am a firm believer in not "throwing the baby out with the bathwater." In other words, while social media can be damaging, it can also be a good thing if used appropriately and sensibly. *There is indeed a good side to social media.* I have been a part of online communities where my faith has grown, and I have seen people unite together in prayer. Many of my favorite Bible teachers and theologians also share daily online. And there have been numerous occasions when I have been very thankful for the ability to spread news quickly.

So how can we keep peace on social media and use it for good?

- **Represent your King well.** Never forget that EVERYTHING you do represents Jesus... that includes everything you say and do online.

- **Know when to keep your mouth shut and your heart open.** This is perhaps the hardest part about social media. Everyone has an opinion, and it's easy to get caught up in expressing your own. While there is certainly a time and place to share your feelings on a particular issue, more often than not, that time and place is not a Facebook comment section. Sometimes it's best to walk in love and keep your comment to yourself.

- **Remember your call to spread Good News.** Our culture is in the habit of sharing bad news... news that inspires people to live in fear rather than hope. *But we are called to something entirely counter-cultural.* I absolutely love the fact that Jesus called the Gospel message "Good News." After all, it is the best news possible!

- **Enjoy the good.** As I said before, social media can be a wonderful tool... *if we're wise in how we use it.* Enjoy it! Keep in touch with friends and family and share the love of Jesus with the world!

Peace on social media is only achieved when we remember that in all things we represent our King.

We need to be careful as children of God not to misrepresent our Father. He is not a God of slander or disunity, but a God of love, joy, and peace beyond all understanding.

HOW TO EXPERIENCE PEACE WHEN THE WORLD IS FALLING APART

The sky is falling! The sky is falling! If you're anything like me, this is exactly how you feel after watching the news. Our world seems to be utterly broken with little to no hope. And as a young woman living in a small town, I feel completely small and helpless. If there isn't a natural disaster, there's a terrorist attack. If there isn't a terrorist attack, there's a mass shooting. And if there isn't a mass shooting, there's a political scandal. *What do we do when the world is falling apart?*

Two key truths to remember when the world is falling apart...

- **Looks can be deceiving...**

Fear sells. It motivates us in a way that nothing else can. This truth is something that news outlets are completely aware of and use as they produce the news for us to watch each day. *(I mean... how many different ways can a terrible situation be analyzed?)* At the same time, it means that good news often falls to the wayside to make room for news people will actually watch.

There was a time when we didn't know every single horrible thing going on in the world. Now we do. Each and every day. On one hand, we can see this as a good thing. After all, change can only occur when we recognize the need to change. But on the other hand, it has caused a lot of us to live in fear. It has also made us feel like the world is spinning off its axis. When in reality, the world has always dealt with terrible tragedies. Just look back at history and statistics. We talk about the 'good old days,' but do we really want to go back to a time when Christians were brutally martyred in arenas as people watched for entertainment? Or how about a time when owning and mistreating slaves was considered normal? We've always had wars. We've always had diseases and famine. And we've always had evil people in the world who did evil things. *Is it really worse now than it was then? Or has sin simply taken on new forms?*

It's definitely something to think about...

But let me challenge you with this: Instead of watching the news in fear, watch the news with hope. In other words, when you read or hear bad news, turn it into an opportunity to pray and trust God. *He is making all things new. And our prayers are a part of that process. Paul said our battle is not against flesh and blood. So as you pray, remember that you are doing battle. You can fight terrorism and evil every time you bow your head to pray.*

- **God's plan to make all things new is a process...**

And he who was seated on the throne said, "Behold, I am making all things new." - Revelation 21:5a

When Jesus came to this earth, He shed light on a lot of dark and ugly places. For example, the Pharisees had long been the religious leaders that everyone looked up to, but Jesus revealed their hearts. He shed His light on injustice as well when He preached about how the poor and helpless were being mistreated.

As the light of Christ permeates this world through us, we will undoubtedly see some ugliness. But rest assured. God is making ALL THINGS new! *And it's a process... one that involves us, the Body of Christ.*

When the world is falling apart (or seems to be), fight in prayer and find rest in the truth that we have an amazing hope for a glorious future in Jesus Christ our Lord!

ENCOUNTERING GOD'S PEACE WHEN YOU'RE EMOTIONALLY TIRED

I have to admit something... *I am emotionally tired.* As I sit here writing, I feel like I'm speaking to myself more than anything. It's hard to cope sometimes when all you want to do is curl up on the couch and sleep. Not from physical exhaustion, but from emotional exhaustion. It's hard to always keep up with life's demands. We have children to raise, houses to clean, jobs to go to, and through it all, we have to maintain healthy relationships with our spouses, family, and friends.

So what are we to do when we are too emotionally tired to get the stuff done that needs to be done?

- **Take your emotions to God.** Being emotionally tired means that at some point your emotions have been (or are currently) on overload. In other words, we tend to feel emotionally exhausted after an emotionally draining experience. So while at the moment, you may feel numb, that feeling is most likely your body's way of shutting down from an emotional strain. For example, I often feel emotionally drained after a difficult day with my children. Raising kids brings up all sorts of emotions. I can feel angry, sad, excited, and even goofy all in a day's work. By the end of the day, my emotions are worn out.

When the Bible says that God longs to be our strength, He isn't just referring to hard times... He longs to be our strength in everything. And He is faithful to be there through the good and the bad.

- **Pray. Pray. And pray some more.** Even when we take our hardships to God, the enemy has a way of reminding us of them. The Bible tells us to persevere for this very reason. *Sometimes trusting God with our problems means that we have to KEEP trusting Him when they resurface. Don't allow the enemy to bring back into your life an issue that you have already taken to God.*

- **Seek help from Scripture.** I can't emphasize this point enough. If I'm being honest, this is a skill that I learned first from my mother. She has had to persevere through many things in her life, and Scripture was key in providing her both strength and encouragement. If you were to see her bedroom and bathroom, you would find Scripture verses printed out and taped to her mirrors. She puts them everywhere as reminders of God's promises in her life.

- **Seek help from a family member.** By family member, I mean a brother or sister in Christ. We are a body of Believers, the family of God. It was His design that we would be relational with one another and that we would lean on each other in times of need... physically and emotionally.

When you're emotionally tired and in desperate need of strength, remember that Jesus promised to be our rest... and He is always faithful.

Unit 5 Study Guide:

1. According to Mark 6:31, what was Jesus' heart towards his disciples' need to rest?

2. Why do you suppose it is important to God for us to rest on a regular basis? (see Mark 2:27)

3. What are some practical ways we can apply Ephesians 4:29 to our social media conversations?

4. Read 1 Corinthians 15:20-28. How does Paul describe the process of everything being put under Jesus' feet and death being defeated?

5. What promise do we find in Psalm 29:11 regarding our emotional well-being?

6. Read Isaiah 40:28-31. What do you learn about God and His heart towards you in this passage?

7. Personal Reflection: What are some practical steps you can personally take to take time for rest in your day-to-day life?

8. Prayer: Read Exodus 33:14. Spend some quality time in God's presence today. Ask Him to be your rest as you go about your day.

Unit 6: Peace in the War Zone of Your Mind

THREE WAYS TO FIGHT FEAR AND REST IN THE PEACE OF GOD

Fear is something that most of us consider to be a normal part of being human. It's a natural emotion, one that we often can't control. From birth, we instinctively feel fear in various situations. Yet, most of us *also* know that fear can be unhealthy and that some fears need to be dealt with head-on. Take, for example, a young child who's afraid to go to school for the first time. It's only natural for that child to be nervous or afraid, but at some point, they will need to face that fear in order to learn and grow. *So how do we fight fear? And how do we know which fears are good for us and which fears will harm us in the long run?*

Here's the truth: The only fear that is good for us is the fear of God. Fear may be a natural human instinct or emotion, but it does not come from Him. In fact, the Bible tells us to not be afraid over 300 times!

Fear is not something that should mark the life of a Believer. While it is something that humans face on a daily basis, we are no longer driven by the "flesh." *We are driven by the power of the Holy Spirit living within us.* We are a new creation. Our old selves lived in fear, but our new selves have nothing to be afraid of... not even death itself.

So if this is all true, why do Christians still feel like fear is a "normal" emotion? It may be normal *apart* from Christ, but it is certainly not "normal" for someone who has been transformed by the Holy Spirit.

If you still find yourself struggling with fear, here are three ways to fight fear once and for all...

- **Identify the REAL enemy and the REAL fight...** Paul reminds us in his letter to the Ephesians that our battle is not against flesh and blood. In other words, our battle is a spiritual one. It is fought on our knees in prayer. Often when we're struggling with fear, we try to find ways to face the thing that scares us. (For example: If you're scared of public speaking, you may try to face your fear by signing up for a public speaking class.) *This is how the world fights fear... but we have the power to fight fear in prayer. And trust me when I say that this is much more effective!*

- **Remember your new identity in Christ...** Do you know who you are? The enemy certainly does. You are a child of God who has been given power and authority in the Holy Spirit. You have powerful weapons at your disposal to tear down strongholds and fight fear and other lies of the enemy. Never forget who God created you to be when you were born again! (And don't forget *Who* you have living within you as well!)

- **Remind the enemy of what's already been done...** When you think of common fears, what comes to mind? Death? Sickness? Failure? Public speaking? Truth be told, Jesus took care of every single one of these fears on the cross. In Him, we inherit eternal life, and we are healed. Victory belongs to us, and the Bible tells us that we are given boldness and words to speak through the power of the Holy Spirit. *We truly have nothing to fear when we are in Christ!*

When you are needing to fight fear in your life, never forget who you are in Christ... because in Him, you truly have nothing to fear!

TRADE YOUR STRESS FOR GOD'S PEACE

Pressure. Tension. Strain. We've all been there... when either the demands of others or the demands we place on ourselves cause stress in our lives. So far, we've dealt with finding God's peace in the chaos of life and when you're emotionally exhausted. *But stress... stress is different.* When I was in college, we were required to take a course on stress management. My main takeaway was that stress is inevitable. It's a part of life. And in the end, it's what we do with stress that matters most.

What if I told you that stress isn't necessarily a bad thing? When we think of stress, our minds often equate it with anxiety or worry. And while it's true that difficult circumstances can cause anxiety, stress is different. It's what we feel when we are under pressure... when life is pushing or pulling us in many different directions... or when our circumstances are too much to carry on our own.

Stress can either damage us or strengthen us.... it all depends on your response.

You see, God uses the trials of life to refine us. They give us opportunities to trust Him and to learn how to rely on His strength rather than our own. When a trial comes our way, we have two choices. **We can allow them to build us up or to break us down.**

So how do you respond when pressure comes your way? How can you trade your stress for God's peace?

- **Identify the problem and take it to God.** When stress happens (and it will), take it to God in prayer. Trust that He will keep His promises and that He will work all things together for good.

- **Maintain a heavenly perspective.** How do you view the world around you? What's your point of view? Paul reminds us in Colossians 3 that we are to set our minds on things above and not focus on the things of this world.

- **Trade your weakness for God's strength.** Stress gives us an amazing opportunity to see God's power at work in our lives. This is why Paul tells us to consider it a joy when trials come our way.

When you trade your stress for God's peace, you are also exchanging your weaknesses for His joy and supernatural strength.

ABIDING IN GOD'S PEACE WHEN YOU'RE AT WAR WITH THE ENEMY

The Bible is clear. There is an enemy, and he has his mind set on destroying your ability to be who God created you to be. He whispers lies, distorts the truth, and attempts to steal your joy and peace any chance he can get. In fact, I think it's safe to say that we're never NOT at war with the enemy. But truth be told, some battles are more difficult than others. I say this from personal experience... some battles are rough.

As children of God, we are called to abide in God's peace no matter what the circumstance. *But how do we abide in peace in the middle of a war?*

Here are three keys to abiding in God's peace in the midst of a spiritual war...

- **Remember that the battle is already won.** Jesus was victorious at the cross. He conquered the power of sin. He defeated death. And He disarmed the enemy. In other words, your war with the enemy is not a fair fight. In fact, he has already lost the war as well as all of his weapons. And you've been armed with the most powerful weapon of all... the truth of Jesus' victory at the cross and the victory you now have in Him.

- **Your job is to stand firm in God's truth.** So if the enemy has already been defeated, what is our role in the battle? Our job is to stand firm and to resist the enemy's lies. He will try to convince you that somehow the battle isn't won. He will try to steal your joy and keep you from your God-given mission here on this earth. But as the Bible tells us, he no longer has any power or weaponry at his disposal. All he can do is hope you will believe his lies. So your job as a believer is to stand firm in God's truth at all times. *In fact, when speaking of our spiritual armor in Ephesians 6, Paul used the phrase "stand firm" three times!*

- **Never forget who you are.** You are a child of God who has been transformed by the power of the Holy Spirit. You are alive in Christ! Not only that, but you are armed and extremely dangerous! You have the sword of truth, and you have been equipped with divine weaponry that has the power to demolish spiritual strongholds.

If you could see your spiritual self for even a moment, you would never again question your ability to stand firm against the enemy!

Knowing and understanding God's truth is essential to abiding in His peace when at war with the enemy.

God did not call us to battle alone. He created us to be strong in Him. He armed us with weaponry that can't possibly lose. And He filled us with His Holy Spirit.

In Him, we are not only unstoppable... we are unbeatable.

ROYALTY IN CHRIST: FINDING REST IN WHO GOD CREATED YOU TO BE

Nearly every little girl dreams of being a princess. We long to feel special, wear gorgeous gowns, walk with authority, and be treated as if we were the most important person in the room. I see this truth in my own two daughters. We have a dress-up trunk full of pretty dresses, tiaras, and tutus. And this desire wasn't taught... they were born with it. From an early age, my girls loved feeling "pretty." To be honest, I'm not entirely sure this longing ever truly goes away. Even as adults, we enjoy being pampered and feeling special from time to time. I have to wonder if this is a God-given desire. *After all, the Bible does speak of our royalty in Christ...*

- **You have been born again into a royal family.** In life, royalty is usually the result of a family relationship... either by blood relationship or by marriage. The same is true in the family of God. The Bible describes our salvation by declaring that we are "born again." We are literally born of the Spirit at the moment we are saved. But the Bible *also* refers to us as the bride of Christ. It is through these relationships (a family bloodline as well as marriage) that we are royalty.

- **You have been given royal authority.** As a member of God's royal family, you have been given all of the rights and responsibilities that come with such a position. And since Jesus defeated the enemy at the cross, you also share in His victory. Jesus, the victorious King of kings, gave us authority as His followers. (Luke 10:19) The Bible tells us that all we have to do is stand firm in God's truth and resist the enemy. *He has no choice but to flee because you are a royal child of God.*

- **You have been given royal duties.** With great power comes great responsibility. Being a follower of Christ is not about sitting around with other Christians simply waiting for Jesus to return. We have a mission to carry out on this earth. *We are here for a divine purpose... a royal purpose! We are called to bring God's light into dark places, to be ambassadors of heaven to the earth, and to live as royal citizens of heaven through the power of God's love.*

Knowing what the Bible says about you and walking in that truth are two different things. Most of us know what the Bible says... we know that God has transformed us into a "nation of royal priests." (1 Peter 2:9) But do we live like royalty? Do we wake up in the morning knowing who we truly are? Do we rest in our God-given identity?

"Her royal highness, Queen (insert your name here)."

What if everyone were to begin addressing you this way? Over time, how would you begin to perceive yourself and your calling in life?

When you begin to see yourself as royalty in Christ Jesus, your demeanor changes. You walk differently, talk differently, and most importantly... love differently.

Unit 6 Study Guide:

1. Read 2 Timothy 1:7, 1 John 4:18, Psalm 56:3-4, and Philippians 4:6. What do you learn about fear from these passages?

2. According to James 1:2-4 and 1 Peter 1:6-7, what should our attitude be towards stressful circumstances? How does this change your thinking?

3. Read Colossians 3:1-2, 12-17. What are some practical ways to apply these verses to your life?

4. How does Colossians 2:15 describe the enemy's defeat? Does this change how you view the enemy? Why or why not?

5. According to 2 Corinthians 10:3-5, what are your weapons as a Believer and what are they capable of doing?

6. Read Revelation 5:9-10. What does this passage say about God's purpose and plan for our lives?

7. Personal Reflection: Take a look at your own life. How do you see yourself? Does this differ from how God sees you?

8. Prayer: Ask God to change your thinking this week and to renew your heart and mind in Him.

Unit 7: God's Plan to Bring Peace to This World

THREE REASONS WHY THE SABBATH IS IMPORTANT IN THE LIFE OF TODAY'S BELIEVER

When God created the world, He rested on the seventh day. The Sabbath day was established in the beginning... before sin and death would enter the world. Fast forward to the days of Moses. In the Ten Commandments, the people of Israel were commanded to never forget the Sabbath day and to keep it holy. Now fast forward once again to the New Testament where Jesus speaks often of the Sabbath and we are told that a Sabbath rest still remains for God's people (Hebrews 4:9) To say that the Sabbath is important to God is an understatement. *Why do you suppose that is? Does God really care about us religiously abstaining from work one day a week? Or is there more to it than that?*

- **The Sabbath is still important today because it is still important to God.** Now, I'm not going to dive into discussing whether or not we should be keeping the Sabbath today as they did in the Old Testament, but I can say with confidence that the Sabbath is an important part of serving God. It is referred to throughout the entirety of God's Word. It was present before the fall of man in the Garden of Eden which also speaks to its importance. Then we have the fourth chapter of Hebrews. In this chapter, we discover what it truly means to enter into God's rest. It was never meant to be honored just one day a week. God's Sabbath rest occurs every single day in the life of a Believer.

- **The Sabbath was always about rest and peace, not religious practice.** God never meant for the Sabbath to become a religious duty or obligation, which is exactly what the Pharisees had turned it into. Jesus made it clear that God created the Sabbath for our benefit, not for His. (Mark 2:27)

- **God designed the Sabbath to foreshadow all we would find in Christ.** When God established the Sabbath in the Garden of Eden, we are told that He "rested" from His work. We all know that God didn't *need* to rest the way we do after a long week... this rest was meant to serve as an example and a foreshadow of what would eventually come. He wanted His people to understand the significance of His peace and rest. *In the end, Jesus is our Sabbath rest. From the very beginning, this was God's intention for His children.*

The Sabbath is important for us today because it is all about Jesus... our source of perfect rest and peace.

THREE REASONS WHY JESUS IS CALLED THE PRINCE OF PEACE

Long before the birth of Jesus, the prophet Isaiah spoke of Him. Wonderful Counselor. Mighty God. Eternal Father. *And Prince of Peace.* So far, we have been discovering what it truly means to abide in God's peace beyond understanding. And I simply couldn't ignore the fact that Jesus is referred to as our Prince of Peace. What does this title mean exactly? And why is it important for us today?

For to us a child is born, to us a son is given; and the government shall be upon his shoulder, and his name shall be called Wonderful Counselor, Mighty God, Everlasting Father, Prince of Peace. Of the increase of his government and of peace there will be no end, on the throne of David and over his kingdom, to establish it and to uphold it with justice and with righteousness from this time forth and forevermore. The zeal of the Lord of hosts will do this.- Isaiah 9:6-7

This Messianic prophecy found in the book of Isaiah describes Jesus in a position of authority. His "government" would be ever increasing, and He would sit on the throne of David forever. While we know that Jesus is the King of kings, these Scriptures speak towards the *nature* of His reign.

- **We serve a King of peace, not chaos.** The world often views our God as anything but peaceful. They point to verses in the Old Testament and use them out of context to make Him seem vengeful and hateful. But this is NOT our Father God! He is a God of peace and order. Simply look at the fruit of the Spirit... *love, joy, peace, patience...* these are the fruit of the Holy Spirit working in our lives *because they specifically describe His nature.* And when God fills our heart, His attributes become apparent in our lives.

For God is not a God of confusion but of peace.... - 1 Corinthians 14:33

- **The mission of Christ was to bring peace to the world.** The death and resurrection of Jesus was always the plan. God longed to transform our chaotic and hateful world into a world filled with His peace and love. And referring to Jesus as the "Prince of Peace" spoke to His mission. He would be the One to finally bring peace to the world.

- **Apart from Him, there is no peace.** This truth goes without saying. Prior to Jesus, the world was far from peaceful. And while we don't have perfect peace yet in terms of our world, what we do have is hope! I love how Isaiah speaks of Jesus' ever-increasing kingdom. Because the truth is that His kingdom is always growing and expanding. God's love and His peace are spreading throughout the entire world. Light is reaching dark places. *And it's so amazing that we get to be a part of it all!*

Peace I leave with you; my peace I give to you. Not as the world gives do I give to you. Let not your hearts be troubled, neither let them be afraid. - John 14:27

Jesus truly is our Prince of Peace.

ENTERING GOD'S REST: HOW TO LIVE IN THE PROMISES OF GOD

When the Israelites were led into the Promised Land, it wasn't easy. In fact, it was downright difficult. They had the promises of God, but they failed time and time again to trust Him. This lack of trust led them to spend forty years wandering the desert. Those who failed to trust God also failed to ever see the Promised Land. It was instead given to their children. In Hebrews 3-4, we read about this very event... only the writer of Hebrews is now using this story as a comparison to what we have in Christ. We have access to God's rest through Jesus. *The question is, will we choose to place our faith in Him... or will we choose to wander?*

Depending on which translation you are reading, Hebrews 4:11 tells us to strive, to labor, or to "do our best" to enter God's rest. We are called to be diligent and put forth an effort. I don't know about you, but this feels a bit odd to me. *We are called to work at entering God's rest?*

Now, this Scripture isn't advocating a works-based faith. In context, it is clear throughout the New Testament that salvation is through our faith in Jesus, not our good works. But what it *is* saying, is that we have to put forth an effort to enter and abide in God's promised rest. We can't just pray a prayer and expect perfect peace to come. *For the Israelites, entering the Promised Land required both trust and obedience to follow God's lead... the same is true for us today.*

Let us therefore strive to enter that rest... - Hebrews 4:11

- **Work *at* rest...** So what does it really mean to strive at entering God's rest? In essence, it means that we do our part. You see, when God gave Israel the Promised Land, He didn't hand it to them on a silver platter. They had to follow Him into the desert. They had to trust Him each and every day to provide their meals and to protect them. And they had to go to war and face enemies, trusting that God would be by their side in battle. *Every time they chose to trust God, He proved His faithfulness.*

Have you done your part to enter God's rest? Have you made the choice to follow Jesus and entrust your life to God?

- **Work *in* rest...** Now, this is the hard part. There are numerous promises found throughout the Bible for God's people. Healing, peace, joy, and strength... just to list a few. But daily living in these promises is a choice. And trust me when I say that the enemy is quick to try and convince you that these promises don't belong to you. (But never forget that they do!)

- **Work *from* rest...** Once you begin to daily abide in God's rest, it becomes second nature. Work no longer feels like work because you are working *from* a place of rest. This was always God's intention for us... to be so at rest in Him that His peace rules in our lives no matter what circumstance the world throws our way.

Entering God's rest isn't enough. He longs for us to live there... to abide in His peace each and every day of our lives.

OUR HOPE FOR PEACE: GOD IS MAKING ALL THINGS NEW

In the book of Revelation, God proclaims, "Behold, I am making all things new." When Jesus came into the world, He established His Kingdom. What began with a small group of disciples, is now growing and expanding to every tribe, tongue, and nation. It is estimated that nearly one-third of the world bows the knee to Jesus. And as chaotic as the world appears sometimes, we can trust that God's plan is at work through the power of the Holy Spirit. We have an amazing hope for peace! *God is indeed making all things new.*

The Kingdom of Heaven is like... Many of Jesus' parables begin this way. He described His Kingdom often throughout His ministry and in many different ways. One way that I find particularly interesting is the concept of a growing Kingdom. He describes it as a "mustard seed" that is planted in a field. And in another parable, it is described as leaven working its way through the dough. (Matthew 13:31, 33)

The very moment sin and death entered the world in the Garden of Eden, God had a plan. He would make all things new. He would take our violent, sinful world and establish a Kingdom where His peace would reign. Nearly every Scripture describing the Kingdom of the Messiah (from both the Old and New Testaments) describes it as a kingdom of peace.

How do you imagine the Garden of Eden? *I imagine the beauty. The peace. And man's ability to walk and talk with God.* When Jesus came to die for mankind, He conquered the power of sin and death. He restored mankind to God so that once again, we could be at peace as we were then.

Looking around at the world today, we aren't surrounded by anything resembling the Garden of Eden... *yet.* But we have hope! The Kingdom of God is growing. Each and every day we are moving towards God's ultimate plan for His people.

And we get to be His hands and feet in the process...

In Christ, we have an amazing hope for peace in this world. God is indeed making all things new!

Unit 7 Study Guide:

1. What do we learn from Hebrews 4:6-11 about God's Sabbath rest?

2. Read Revelation 21:1-8 and 22:1-5. How is Jesus' Kingdom of peace described in its fullness?

3. How does Isaiah 11:1-10 describe our King and His Kingdom?

4. According to Matthew 11:28-29, what is required of us to enter God's rest?

5. What additional truths do we learn about our future hope and Sabbath rest from Isaiah 65:17-25?

6. Read Matthew 13:44-46. What truths do we learn about the Kingdom of God and its value from Jesus our King?

7. Personal Reflection: What peace do you gain from knowing and understanding God's plan for His people? How does this change your thinking as well as your decision making?

8. Prayer: Looking around at the world today, it's easy to feel like peace is no where in sight. Spend some time in prayer this week asking God to continually remind you of His plan. Never forget... there remains a Sabbath rest for God's people!

Unit 8: Sharing God's Peace With the World

THE GOSPEL OF PEACE: GOD'S PLAN TO SAVE THE WORLD

If you were to ask someone what their greatest wish was for mankind, "world peace" would probably be near the top of their wish list. We crave peace in our lives, in our homes, and in our communities. Yet, for some reason, many of us have resigned ourselves to the fact that we may never see such peace in our lifetimes. This world is simply a chaotic, crazy place with evil people in it. Even nature itself seems to be in on the chaos... hurricanes, tornadoes, and other natural disasters threaten our peace continually. So when the Bible speaks of peace, we often push it forward in time. We tell ourselves that peace is for the future, not for the here and now. *We will have peace someday... right?*

God does have a plan for peace in this world, one that we actively get to be a part of as we spread the Good News of His Kingdom far and wide. But that doesn't mean we have to wait for peace.

Here and now, we can experience His peace beyond all understanding. Because of the cross, we can abide in it each and every day, and this peace is made available through Jesus. It is only when the Holy Spirit dwells within us that we can experience a supernatural peace that comes from God alone.

Our access to the peace of God is the result of our salvation... it comes once we place our faith in Jesus.

To the woman who anointed Jesus' feet with expensive perfume...

> **And he said to the woman, "Your faith has saved you; go in peace." - Luke 7:50**

To the woman who touched the hem of Jesus' garment and was healed...

> **And he said to her, "Daughter, your faith has made you well; go in peace." - Luke 8:48**

I love the imagery in the above passages! Both women were made whole. They came to Jesus with unrest in their lives both physically and emotionally, and He miraculously healed them. They were then able to go in peace. But like us today, they had a choice. Jesus had given them His peace, but they had to "go" and walk in that peace.

The Good News of Jesus is referred to as the Gospel of Peace in Ephesians 6. *Why?* Because after centuries of unrest, peace had finally come into the world. And we get to announce this good news of peace to the entire world!

In Jesus...

- **We have peace with God...** No longer are we far away from God. We can be close to Him, be in His presence anytime, anyplace. And it's not just the fact that we have been made holy, but also that we have been born again as sons and daughters. He is our Father, and we are His kids.

- **We have peace in our hearts...** Nothing can separate us from the love of God. *Nothing.* We are secure in our salvation. It's a done deal. And above and beyond that, we have the Holy Spirit in our lives who strengthens us and give us His peace even in our own moments of weakness.

- **We have hope for peace in this world...** Our job is to spread the Gospel of Peace to the world. *Jesus is King! And His Kingdom is here and ever growing!* And one day He will return and all will be made new in the twinkling of an eye.

In Jesus, we can experience peace beyond understanding in every area of our lives. This truly is the Gospel of Peace.

DON'T WORRY, BE HAPPY:
HOW TO ABIDE IN GOD'S PEACE IN EVERY CIRCUMSTANCE

Don't worry. Be happy. As simple as it sounds, most of us know that it's hard not to worry sometimes. And happiness isn't always easy to come by either. But what if I said that there was some biblical truth to this well-known saying? According to Scripture, it is possible to experience peace in every circumstance of life. And Jesus instructed us not to worry, but to trust that God is a good Father who provides for His children.

Paul had peace no matter what life threw his way. Even when some tried to stone him to death for preaching the Gospel, he found reasons to rejoice in all God was doing. (Acts 14:19-28) He often had no idea where he would be sleeping at night or where his next meal would come from, yet he wrote:

...For I have learned in whatever situation I am to be content. I know how to be brought low, and I know how to abound. In any and every circumstance, I have learned the secret of facing plenty and hunger, abundance and need. I can do all things through him who strengthens me. - Philippians 4:11-13

Here are three key takeaways from Paul's life when it comes to living a life of peace…

- **Complete trust in God to provide…** It's difficult to worry when you have complete trust in God. In fact, it's impossible. Worry is simply the result of a lack of trust. Let me put it this way. My children are young and have complete trust in their parents to provide for them. They don't worry whatsoever about food, clothing, shelter… the basic needs of life. In these areas of their lives, there is complete peace.

Do you trust God as your Father to work everything together for good? Do you trust Him to provide for your needs?

- **Contentment in all that God has provided…** Contentment is a funny thing. Paul spoke of being content in both richness and poverty. Truth be told, I almost think it's harder to be content in wealth. We live in a culture that always wants more… the next "latest and greatest" thing.

What would happen if we lived in such a way that we were truly content in every circumstance? How would this affect our ability to experience peace in our lives?

- **Confidence in who God is and that His plan will prevail…** Paul knew beyond the shadow of a doubt that God's will would be carried out to completion… that God would be glorified no matter what happened to him in this life. (Philippians 1:20-21)

When we commit ourselves to the truth that to live is Christ and to die is gain, we will experience God's peace in every circumstance of our life.

LESSONS FROM PSALM 23: HOW TO WALK IN THE PEACE OF GOD

If anyone knew unrest and difficult circumstances, it was David. Yet, he was a man after God's own heart, and he knew how to walk in the peace of God. One of David's most well-known psalms is none other than Psalm 23. When I think of peace, this particular psalm isn't usually the first to come to mind. Yet, reading it now, I can clearly see the genuine peace David had in his heart... a peace that only could have come from knowing God deeply and personally.

The Lord is my shepherd; I shall not want. - Psalm 23:1

When we trust Jesus to meet all of our needs (as He promised He would), we learn to be content in whatever situation we find ourselves in... *we do not want for anything.*

He makes me lie down in green pastures. He leads me beside still waters. - Psalm 23:2

Not only does Jesus meet all of our needs, He takes us where we need to be. (And I don't know about you, but green pastures and quiet waters sound rather amazing!)

He restores my soul. He leads me in paths of righteousness for his name's sake.- Psalm 23:3

Jesus breathes life into our souls and directs our lives as He works all things together for good.

Even though I walk through the valley of the shadow of death, I will fear no evil, for you are with me; your rod and your staff, they comfort me. - Psalm 23:4

David found himself in many situations that could be described as "the valley of the shadow of death," but God was always with him. David never encountered danger alone. And not only was God with him, but he found comfort in knowing that God would discipline him and guide his life in a way that only a loving Father could.

You prepare a table before me in the presence of my enemies; you anoint my head with oil; my cup overflows. - Psalm 23:5

I love this imagery... imagine God setting before you a banquet. Oh... and all of your enemies are there. In David's case, his enemies more than likely wanted to kill him. Yet God demonstrated to these men that David belonged to him.

God blessed David and demonstrated favor in front of his enemies. And He has done the same for us. (It's why the enemy hates us so much.) We are truly blessed, and God has shown us His favor by adopting us as His own children and by giving us His Holy Spirit to empower our lives.

Surely goodness and mercy shall follow me all the days of my life, and I shall dwell in the house of the Lord forever.- Psalm 23:6

This is the ultimate peace... dwelling in God's presence forever and ever. And this peace isn't simply for the future, we can experience His presence now in our day-to-day lives. Anytime, anywhere... we have access to our heavenly Father.

David demonstrated throughout his life that even when we walk through the valley of the shadow of death, we can walk in the peace of God.

HOW TO LIVE YOUR LIFE AS A PEACEMAKER

What exactly is a "peacemaker"? When I was younger, I always envisioned someone who was able to restore peace... someone who was good at mediating difficult situations... or someone who understood the art of compromising. But is this what Jesus meant when He challenged us to be peacemakers?

"Blessed are the peacemakers, for they shall be called sons of God." - Matthew 5:9

The Greek word Jesus used in this passage was *eirēnopoios*, which simply means to love and promote peace. *But what does this look like in action? How does one practically make peace?*

- **A peacemaker lives in peace with everyone around them...** The Bible tells us to live in harmony with everyone in our lives to the best of our ability. The key phrase here being "to the best of our ability." (Romans 12:17-18) So as a peacemaker, have you done *everything you can* to create peace in your relationships? Are there areas of unforgiveness and unrest?

- **A peacemaker spreads the peace of Christ to the world...** Jesus is referred to as the Prince of Peace. He came to conquer sin and death and to bring His kingdom of peace into the world. And it is our job as God's children to spread the news of His peace to the far corners of the earth.

In this way, we make peace... by bringing God's peace to places that have never encountered it.

- **A peacemaker lives in such a way that their peace is contagious...** God has really been challenging me personally in this particular area. We speak often of how joy can be contagious. But did you know peace is contagious as well? Think about it this way, when you are around someone who is truly content with their lives... someone who allows nothing to steal that peace from them... how do you feel? Do you long to experience the peace they have found?

The truth is that we all crave peace. I think we long for contentment in our lives even more than we long for happiness. Because in the end, when we are content, we are happy. So when we walk in the power of God's peace each and every day of our lives (and I mean truly walk in it), the world around us will understand just what it means to be a citizen of the Kingdom.

We can't preach peace to the world and live in a place of unrest. If we're going to be peacemakers, we have to learn to abide in God's peace. Only then can we share His peace with the world.

A peacemaker lives a radical life full of God's peace... which is far beyond the world's understanding. And in this way, their peace becomes contagious to everyone around them.

I challenge you with this... Go. Walk in the peace of God no matter what life throws your way. Be someone who makes peace everywhere you go. God has healed you, restored you, and made you whole through the power of the Holy Spirit. He has given you access to His peace beyond the world's understanding.

So recklessly abandon your worldly thoughts, attitudes, and concerns... and as Jesus said, go in peace.

Unit 8 Study Guide:

1. According to Isaiah 52:7, what are we called to announce as we spread the Good News to the world around us?

2. What do we learn about contentment in 1 Timothy 6:6-8? How does contentment bring about peace in our lives?

3. Read 1 Samuel 19:8-12. Some scholars believe Psalm 23 was written during this chaotic time in David's life. How does this affect your view of this famous psalm? What can we learn from David's peace in this situation?

4. Romans 14:19 tells us to "pursue the things which make for peace." What are some practical ways we can implement this in our lives today?

5. Read Proverbs 3:5-6. What does this passage have to do with "reckless abandon"? What promise are we given for surrendering it all to God?

6. Describe what it means to you personally to live a life of reckless abandon and to dwell in the peace of God.

7. Personal Reflection: Make a list of any thoughts, feelings, or concerns you are currently hanging on to in your life. What steps do you plan to take to surrender these things to God?

8. Prayer: Using Psalm 23 as a guide, spend some time in prayer thanking God for His perfect peace and provision.

ABOUT THE AUTHOR

Alyssa J Howard is a wife and mom to two young girls. She lives with her family in the Pacific Northwest where she loves to bake, run, drink coffee, and play with her daughters. Alyssa first fell in love with writing while earning her Master of Arts degree in theological studies through Liberty Theological Seminary, and she has been writing about Jesus and the Christian life for the past four years at alyssajhoward.com. She is the author of *Renewed and Transformed: A Study in What It Means to Live with the Mind of Christ*, and she has also worked as part of the content editing team as well as the Bible study writing team for Hello Mornings (hellomornings.org).

Made in the USA
Coppell, TX
17 June 2020